I Need to Preach NOW!

A Short Guide to Preparing and Delivering an Expository Message

Ben Trahan

I Need to Preach Now

ISBN: 9798374021899

Dedication

This work is dedicated first and foremost to Jesus Christ, the only God and Savior

To my wife, Julianne

To our children, Sean & Gianna

and to those who mentored me,
James Harmeling,
the late Tom Givens,
& Dan Smouse

Table of Contents

Introduction

"And He gave the apostles, the prophets, the evangelists, the shepherds and teachers, to equip the saints for the work of ministry, for building up the body of Christ,"

-Ephesians 4:11-12

How can a new Sunday School teacher, youth volunteer, small group leader or novice preacher be equipped to accurately teach the Bible in the quickest way possible so they can effectively begin serving NOW instead of months from now? This booklet was developed to address that very issue.

Many great books have already been written devoting hundreds of pages to the art of expository preaching and teaching such as *Christ-Centered Preaching* by Brian Chapel, *Biblical Preaching* by Haddon W. Robinson, and *Introduction to Expository Preaching* by John MacArthur. I have read them all, gone through them with others, and highly encourage you to do the same if you have not done so already. But for those just starting on the journey, or training others that are, I offer this short booklet summarizing the preparation and delivery of an expository message as a first step in the process. I have used the contents in various forms over the past 30 years to equip those who served alongside me. Knowing you are more likely to retain a volunteer that is actively serving compared to one that is passively observing, it is my hope and prayer that it will quickly get you and/or those who serve with you immediately in the trenches preparing and sharing expository messages as it has done for many others. May it also serve as a reminder of the process, keeping you pointed in the right direction as you continue to teach God's Word and develop the gift He has given you.

The Delivery

The delivery of an expository message has essentially four parts: Introduction, Transition, Body, and Conclusion. Without any delay, let's look at each of these parts separately.

Introduction

The purpose of the introduction is to take a person's mind off what they are currently thinking and prepare them to listen to what you are about to preach. People's minds can be literally anywhere! Thankfully, some are just waiting to hear what God's word has to say! Others are thinking of how great the praise worship just was (or wasn't). Still others are thinking of the fight they just had with a family member or friend before they arrived, or what they are going to do after the message is done. The task you need to accomplish with the introduction is to bring everybody from these vastly different places and focus them on what God is about to say to them through the preaching/teaching of His word.

Unfortunately, statistics show if you do not grab someone's attention within the first 30 seconds, you have basically lost them for the duration of the message. Mature listeners will give you a little more grace, about 90 seconds worth. When you understand the purpose and importance of the introduction, it is frightening to be sure, but not impossible. Do not forget the power of prayer here! Always pray for God's supernatural influence to focus people on His word.

Many things can be used as an introduction.

- Stories/Pictures – fact or fiction, humorous or serious, it just needs to grab everyone's attention quickly AND begin to introduce the main point of the message.
- Video clips – just make sure the main point you want people to pick up on is clearly communicated, either in the clip or through your own introduction or summary of the clip. Do

not allow too much lead-in time to the main point or people are likely to lose focus and tune out.

- Music – special music performed, or the last worship song sung before you speak can be used to introduce the main point of the text. Restate the main point or lyric of the song as you go into the Transition.
- Review – If you are preaching or teaching a series, remind everyone where you left off last time. Reiterate the main points and applications from the previous teaching times in an interesting and creative way.

Transition – Tell them what you are going to say

Now that you have everyone's attention, it is time to spell out why it is imperative that people listen to what God's word is about to say for the next 20, 30, 40, 60 or more minutes. Remember, the goal of preaching/teaching God's word is ***life change***. Whether this means presenting the gospel to a lost sinner in order that they become saved, or preaching God's truth to mold a redeemed saint more into the image of our Savior, this is where you must complete the statement, "Because God's Word says _______________, you and I must _______________." Here you state the main point of the passage in such a way that a person's need for and direction of change is clear. Supporting details of the text may also be stated here, but DO NOT simply state the facts of the passage.

Body – Say what the text says

Here is the main part of the message. This is where you show your listeners what the text says and how it applies to their lives. You explain the main point, go through the text verse by verse, explain the supporting details and subpoints, give clarifying illustrations and suggested life applications for each point. The importance of knowing the outline of the passage cannot be understated here.

Conclusion - Tell them what the text said

In the Conclusion, you restate in summary form the main point and sub-points of the passage with a heavy emphasis on life application, giving specific examples of what needed changes could or should look like. Do not simply restate the facts of the passage and think that is an adequate conclusion. Do not make applications so brief or vague that a person walks away from the message unclear about what God wants them to do. Complete the statement, "Because God's word says ____________________, you and I must _________________."

The Preparation

Hopefully the delivery of an expository message is very familiar to you. I hope you have grown up under a solid teaching ministry and have heard many great expository messages modeled. You may even be remembering some of those messages and now seeing the structure that was carefully, thoughtfully, and deliberately crafted into them. However, while you deliver an expository message beginning with the Introduction, followed by the Transition, then the Body, and finally the Conclusion, the preparation of these parts is in a different order entirely: Body → Conclusion → Transition → Introduction.

Why is an expository message prepared in a different order than it is delivered? Because the text (Body) dictates what the application (Conclusion) will be. The application becomes the "why" people need to listen to the text (Transition). Once the "why" is known, you can now develop a targeted Introduction that grabs people's attention and quickly leads them to the "why" they need to listen. The expository message takes its direction and meaning out of the text (exegesis) and lets the Bible speak for itself. You and I do not put our own ideas into the text (isogesis) and make the Bible say what we want it to say.

The first and most essential step in preparing an expository message is prayer. Before you even look at the text, pray for the wisdom to understand it. James 1:5 tells us, "If any of you lacks wisdom, let him ask God, who gives generously to all without reproach, and it will be given him." Understand that the message you will be sharing is not yours. It is God's. Ask the Author of Scripture to reveal that message to you from His Word and believe He will as He has promised. This cannot be emphasized enough. Pray! And pray every step of the way!

Body – What does the text say?

The body is the heart of the message. As much as possible you must not come to the text thinking you already know what it says. AVOID COMMENTARIES AND STUDY BIBLE NOTES until after you outline the passage! Do your best to read the text like it was your very first time. Read each word carefully. Look up words you do not know, in the original language if possible.

Original Language Study Tools:

- Vine's Expository Dictionary of Old & New Testament Words is a great tool for looking up words.
- An Interlinear Bible contains the original text above each line of English text, with each word keyed to Strong's numbers so you know exactly which word to look up in Vine's or a Greek/Hebrew lexicon, as well as being able to see the original word order. Why is word order important? When you are teaching from the New Testament, one of the beautiful things about the Greek language is that it puts the main ideas at the beginning of a sentence. Whenever you have a question as to what the main idea of a verse or sentence is, look it up in the Interlinear and see what is said first. Don't have one? Not to worry. The New American Standard Bible (NASB) does a great job of translating the original text and maintaining most of the original word order. Unfortunately, word order is not as important in Hebrew. Just like in English, you can rearrange words in a Hebrew sentence a few different ways and not change the meaning of the sentence.

The main focus here is that you need to understand the words in the same way the original author and recipients understood them. Only then can you hope to properly apply them to yourself and those you teach in our day and age.

As you read the text, use what is called the Literal-Grammatical-Historical method of interpreting the text (Hermeneutics). Let's break these down.

- Literal - We make the assumption that God gave and preserved His word for us in order to communicate clearly to us. When the Bible says in 1 Samuel 17:40 that David picked up five smooth stones from the brook and placed them in his pouch, it means that David picked up five smooth stones from the brook and placed them in his pouch! Earth shattering, I know! The five stones do not symbolize five ways to tackle difficult problems in life, or five principles of leadership, or five things we must have to prepare for spiritual warfare (and yes, messages have been preached on these topics and many other groups of five things from this text). Words have meaning. God moved the authors of the Bible to use specific words for the specific meanings they have. What about poetry? What about prophecy? I'm glad you asked.
- Grammatical - Not only did God move the authors to use certain words, He also moved them to put them together in a certain way. Much of the Bible is written in narrative, a straightforward telling of events and ideas. If this is how the passage is constructed, the plain sense of the text is the intended meaning. However, the Bible also uses poetic and prophetic language. It uses metaphors and similes. Jesus spoke in parables where He clearly was using one thing to symbolize another. If the grammar of a passage uses obvious figurative and symbolic language, then we have to take into account what is being symbolized. The grammar dictates it.
- Historical - Finally, we must understand what the author was trying to communicate to his original audience. I already stated the importance of knowing the meaning of words in their original language. Historical context takes our understanding one step further. What is the setting of the narrative passage? What are the cultural meanings of

certain phrases and actions? A good commentary or book on Bible customs and cultures will help you here. To stress the importance of this, let us look at one very real example of how different theologies have been developed because a well-known gospel event was taken out of its historical context.

The Last Supper

We are all familiar with the Last Supper in the synoptic Gospels (Matt. 26, Mark 14, Luke 22) and the establishment of the Communion celebration. The question we are going to apply our Literal-Grammatical-Historical hermeneutic to is: What did Jesus mean when He said "this is My body" and "this is My blood" to the disciples? Three prominent interpretations exist today:

- Transubstantiation – the bread and wine literally become Christ's body and blood during the Communion celebration.
- Consubstantiation – Jesus' presence is in the bread and wine. They do not literally become Jesus' body and blood, but they are more than just symbols.
- Memorial – the bread and wine are just symbols to remind us of Jesus' death on the cross.

Supporters of Transubstantiation take the passage completely literally. They will point out that Jesus said, "This IS my body. This IS my blood." Grammatically, the texts are narrative, describing an actual, historical event, not a parable or fictional story. So the completely literal and grammatical understanding of the text would be that the bread and wine literally become Jesus' flesh and blood. This would be the proper understanding IF the historical context did not have anything to contribute.

In addition to applying literal and grammatical hermeneutics, supporters of the Memorial viewpoint also take the historical context into account. They will point out that the Last Supper took place in the historical context of the Passover meal, a meal where every food and drink and action was a symbol meant to remind Israel of the details of the Exodus. Within this meal of symbols, Jesus takes the unleavened bread and probably the 3rd of the four cups of wine drank during the meal, the Cup of Redemption, and gives them a new symbolic meaning relating to Himself and His upcoming death on the cross that would accomplish our redemption from sin. Understanding the historical context, that the Last Supper was a Passover meal, a meal of memorial symbols, shows that the disciples would have understood Jesus to be redefining those symbols, not making statements about any supernatural transformation of the bread and wine (of course, God could do that if He so chose). If that is what the disciples would have understood, that is the proper interpretation. Context is everything: literally, grammatically, and historically!

Not to be left out, supporters of Consubstantiation do not believe that the bread and wine literally become Christ's body and blood, but do believe that Christ's presence is in them during the Communion celebration. This view has no textual support. It does not take the passage literally. It spiritualizes the grammar of a historical narrative. It does not take the historical context into account. Consubstantiation would seem to be a human invention that seeks to be a middle ground between Transubstantiation and the Memorial view.

See how important historical context is?

<u>Outline</u> - Now that you understand all the details of the text, outline the passage showing its main point and supporting points and details. An expository message should only have one main point which should fill in the first blank of the message focus: Because God's Word says **(<u>main point of passage</u>)**, you and I must ______________." Every other point and detail in the passage must support the main point. If you have two main points, you will be preaching two messages at the same time. This is both difficult to do and difficult for your hearers to follow. Cut your text down to one main point and save the other for another message.

<u>Check the Commentaries</u> – Now it is time to check your work. Hopefully you own or have access to good commentaries. Read three or four different commentaries and compare them to your study. Hopefully you will be encouraged, seeing how God has lead you to the same conclusions as other godly believers. Commentaries often provide you with just a little more depth to your study, a better way to explain a point, or a great illustration. You might even discover something you overlooked.

That being said, if you have come up with something that no one else seems to be saying, you need to seriously reconsider your work. It is highly unlikely that you will have discovered something that literally thousands of godly people have missed for thousands of years. Possible? Yes. Probable? No.

Application - Once you have outlined the main point, supporting points and details, supplemented by the commentators, seek to answer the second blank of the message focus, starting with the main point and continuing with each supporting point. Because God's Word says (point of passage), you and I must **(application of point)**." Look at the text and ask yourself the question, "So what?" Brian Chapel in his book *Christ Centered Preaching* quoted David Veerman who said, "Preachers make a fundamental mistake when they assume that by providing parishioners with biblical information the people will automatically make the connection between scriptural truth and their everyday lives." Remember, the goal of the expository message is life change! James 1:22 implores us, "But **be doers of the word**, and not hearers only, deceiving yourselves." In addition, Paul warns us in 1 Corinthians 8 that knowledge without application in love leads to sinful pride. Communicating Bible facts is useless without life application.

Illustration - Each supporting point not only needs an application, it also needs an illustration in order to relate them to something your listeners already understand. This is exactly what Jesus did with parables. He used things that 1st century people in Israel were already familiar with (mustard seeds, planting, harvesting, weddings, etc.) and related spiritual truths to them (faith, witnessing, being prepared).

Illustrations also allow your hearers to catch a "mental breather" during the message. You may have just spent 10-15 minutes on some deep theology. It has taken your hearers a lot of focused effort to stay on track with you. Giving an illustration allows them to relax their minds a little, absorb what they just heard, and prepare for the next "deep" part of the text.

What can you use to illustrate your messages?

- More Scripture – the use of familiar Bible passages to illustrate Scripture not only helps your hearers understanding, it also has other beneficial side effects. 1) It demonstrates the unity of the Bible, 2) It shows the connection between the Old and New Testaments, 3) It brings new understanding to the text used for the illustration. If your New Testament passage makes a reference to an Old Testament passage, use it! If your Old Testament passage contains a prophecy that is fulfilled in the New Testament, use it! Illustrating Scripture with Scripture is a win-win!

- Stories - there is no lack of stories that can be used for illustration. Sources include your personal life, well-known history, well-known fiction, even jokes.
- Media - movies, television, books, and music are part of our culture and provide many illustrations. Consider showing video clips, reading an excerpt, or playing part or all of a song. Be aware that the use of a certain piece of media may be taken as your endorsement of its source. If that is not the case, go out of your way to let your audience know that you do not approve of the movie, show, book, or artist.
- Current events - keep in touch with what's going on in the world. The plethora of news outlets and social media provide many illustrations people are currently aware of. Using current events also helps demonstrate how the Bible still applies to us today.

If you have not already, develop a way to collect good illustration ideas. Use a system that works for you, whether hard copy files or digital. There are also many online resources that provide good message illustrations.

Create a Message Outline – This is the outline you will use to preach/teach from. It is different from the passage outline you created earlier. Plug your application points and illustrations into your passage outline. Often it will follow the flow of the passage (verse 1, supporting point, illustration, application, verse 2, supporting point, application, illustration, verse 3, etc…), but not always. Sometimes it is better to teach verses 7-9 before you cover verses 1-6. For example, when I teach 2 Peter 1:3-11, I personally prefer to teach vs. 10-11 before verses 3-9 because it is the "why" of verses 3-9. If you are thinking about switching the order, make sure you have a really, really good reason to. Scripture was written in a certain order for a specific reason. Make sure you understand it!

Conclusion - What did the text say?

The conclusion of your message is where you restate the main point, supporting points and applications, **with a heavy focus on specific applications**. Think of it as a summary of what you just taught. You may feel silly saying the same thing three times (remember: tell them what you're going to say, say it, tell them what you said) but just remember, studies have shown that most people must hear something seven times before they will actually remember it. The use of visuals cuts down the number of times you need to repeat, but they do not eliminate it. You may want to think about using some additional repetition in the body of your message as you move from point to point (Point #1 was __________, point #2 was __________, now Point #3 is…).

Be sure you are even more specific with the message applications you gave in the body of your message. You are aiming for life change here. Give your hearers many ideas (without going overboard) to help them apply what they just heard to their own personal lives. Is your audience a mixture of children, young adults, adults, senior citizens, men and women? Make sure you give application points specific to each group. Don't exclude anyone. Know your audience!

Transition - What you are going to say

You are on the home stretch! Most of the hard work is now done! Now that you know what the passage says and how it will apply to your hearers, it's time to prepare them for what they are about to hear, and more importantly, tell them *why* they need to listen to you. This can often be accomplished by turning your main application points into questions or by stating the specific "problem" situation(s) the message will address. The transition needs to raise important issues people are or should be thinking about. As you deliver your transition, your hearers should be saying to themselves, "I've wondered about that" or asking themselves, "Why haven't I thought about that?" Now that they see the important issue(s) the message will address, tell them the main point of the message and give a broad response application of that truth as you prepare to show them all the important details and specific applications from the text.

Introduction - Grab their attention!

The final step! Compared to everything you have done so far, this is the easy part! But do not mistake easy for unimportant. Remember, if you do not grab your audience's attention in the first 30 to 90 seconds, you have most likely lost them for the entire message. The introduction needs to take your hearers from wherever they happen to be mentally into the transition of your message. Whatever you choose to open with, in one way or another, it needs to begin to introduce the main point of the message or the issue it addresses. We already covered things that can be used for introduction in "The Delivery" section at the beginning of this booklet, but please do not feel limited to that list. Be creative! Be unexpected! But most importantly, be interesting! Grab their attention!

It is Finished!

That's it! In a nutshell, this is how to prepare and deliver an expository message. Like playing a guitar (or most instruments for that matter), the basics can be leaned quickly but it takes a lifetime to master. Again, many good books have been written on this subject in much greater depth, some of which I listed in the Forward of this booklet. I highly encourage you to read one or more of them. The two goals of this booklet are to quickly get you and others in your ministry started properly preparing and delivering expository messages and to serve as a periodic reminder of the processes. To that end, the following is a diagram to keep in mind for every message you prepare and deliver from now on:

The Expository Message

Delivery: Intro → Transition → Body → Conclusion
Preparation: Body → Conclusion → Transition → Intro

Focus: Because God's Word says ___________,
you and I must ______________________.

May God richly bless you and the multitude of lives you will impact for God's glory through the faithful preaching of His Word!

About the Author

Pastor Ben Trahan is a graduate of The Master's College in Santa Clarita, CA, and has served in vocational ministry since 1993 shepherding children, youth and adults. Married in 1995 to his wife, Julianne, they have raised a son and a daughter to adulthood who, by the grace of God, were saved at young ages and continue to walk with the Lord.

www.ingramcontent.com/pod-product-compliance
Lightning Source LLC
LaVergne TN
LVHW010515160826
845677LV00012B/2860

* 9 7 9 8 3 7 4 0 2 1 8 9 9 *